Brian B. Kim

Stock Market IQ & EQ

The Vital, Fun, and Concisely Definitive Introduction to Investing

Six Paradoxes of Investing

&

Why we do so poorly in stocks
The dominant strategy
Analyzing stocks like Benjamin Graham
How to responsibly trade stocks
The question we must always ask
Deciding not to invest
Where the market stands today

ISBN-10: 0-9909089-2-5
ISBN-13: 978-0-9909089-2-0

ALSO BY BRIAN B. KIM

Trading Stocks Using Classical Chart Patterns:
A Complete Tactical & Psychological Guide
for Beginners and Experienced Traders

For M.

CONTENTS

PART I
WHAT WE ARE UP AGAINST

Chapter 1 A Fresh Perspective 3
Chapter 2 Our Record 7
Chapter 3 Buy High and Sell Low... 11
Chapter 4 Experts Do Not Have Expertise 17

PART II
THE "SIMPLE RULES" FOR INVESTING:
THEN THERE IS REAL LIFE

Chapter 5 What We Are Supposed To Do But Cannot........................ 21
Chapter 6 First Challenge: Picking the Boring Index Fund 23
Chapter 7 Second Challenge: Patience (And Mind Tricks)................... 27
Chapter 8 Third Challenge: Ignoring Others 35

PART III
OTHER APPROACHES TO THE STOCK MARKET

Chapter 9   Picking Stocks 41
Chapter 10 Trading Stocks... 59
Chapter 11 Staying Away from Stocks... 65

PART IV
ADDITIONAL TOOLS

Chapter 12 Past Performance Does Not Guarantee Future Results.
Or Does it? 71
Chapter 13 We Must Always Ask This Question 79

PART V
FINAL THOUGHTS

Chapter 14 First We Must Do This...89
Chapter 15 Conclusion..91

About the Author 93
Disclaimer 95

PART I

What We Are Up Against

Chapter 1
A Fresh Perspective

<u>Why we need a different approach</u>

This book is meant to be an enjoyable, useful, and invigorating introduction to the stock market. I strove to make the book not only clear but also compelling by including many distinct and "ah ha" pieces of knowledge with which to approach the market.

One of the distinguishing features of this book is that it does not assume we will "buy and hold" and benefit from the wonders of compound interest. Too many books tempt the reader by saying something like: *If you start with $5,000 in an index fund in your 20s and then put in just $1,500 a year for the next 40 years, your money will grow to $1 million because stocks average a 10% return every year.*

This statement is dangerously incomplete. For example, while stocks have returned 10% a year over some stretches, that does not mean we earn 10% every year. If so, then more people might succeed as investors although—even then—there is no guarantee. Instead, stock returns vary year to year: stocks can go up 32% (as they did in 2013) or down 22% (2002) or 37% (2008). And we unerringly buy after a 30% up year and sell after a 40% down year. ***Quite simply, we are unable to "buy and hold."*** But since steady investing sounds simple and attractive enough, millions of people get into stocks and assume a smooth and quick road to wealth. Soon we realize "buying and holding" is not so straightforward and that stocks can go down—a lot. So we panic and sell for a loss, again and again. To avoid this outcome, we must better understand the market, ourselves, and our task.

We will roam

Another way this book is different is that it acknowledges that many of us will speculate. We may call it something else, but if we buy a stock on a hunch or on a friend's "recommendation" or because it is "supposed to go up," we are speculating. Since many of us are interested in picking and trading stocks, and as we are likely to pick and speculate without much sense of the risks involved, we will discuss how we might intelligently pick individual stocks (Chapter 9) and responsibly trade stocks (Chapter 10). It is unrealistic to assume that warning "don't speculate" will suffice. So we'll learn about the risks and realities of picking and trading stocks so that we can make an informed decision.

We have a choice

Finally, this book is different because it is not a one-way guide to getting *in* stocks even though I strived to give the best overall introduction. It also explains the reasonableness of getting *out* of or *not investing* in stocks depending on our financial goals and self-assessment. It is about the choice that comes from knowledge, the freedom to walk our own path, and the maturity and wisdom to not worry about what others are doing.

Why discuss the option of not investing?

Because it is so very easy to lose money in the stock market.

But if the market is so dangerous, then why not just write a book urging people to avoid stocks? For two reasons.

First, the stock market is a way—though not an easy one—to compound our savings over the long run. While Americans justifiably directed their anger at Wall Street and financial institutions for their role in the financial crisis of 2007 to 2009, a greater proportion of Americans own stocks than citizens of most other rich countries. And Americans who have stayed the course with their stock investment for 20, 30, and 40 years have done well.

Second, the stock market, for better and for worse, occupies a large place in the American psyche. The stock market, for better and for worse, is one of the defining institutions of America. It is not America, but it is a significant part of it. And tens of millions of Americans, for better and for worse, are in the stock market. And millions more are thinking about investing in stocks.

So I wrote this book to be a clear and interesting resource for those seeking a useful and original perspective on investing.

If you are already in the stock market, then this book will give you the information to make you a better investor or, perhaps, a former investor who has decided that the stock market is not for you.

If you are thinking about investing in stocks, then this book will give you the facts to help you make an informed decision.

Whatever our situation, we will find candor and relentless calls to think for ourselves. While this book has a cautionary tone, the goal is not to scare or be gloomy but to help and be useful.

Timeless themes

In our journey, we will encounter the following paradoxes of investing:

6 Paradoxes of Investing

- Good investing is more about doing nothing than doing something.

- Past performance does not guarantee future results, but history is a useful guide.

- Emotional control is more important than high intelligence. The smarter we are, the more difficult investing is likely to be.

- At the end of this book, we will know more about stocks and investing than almost everyone, including (especially?) most stock brokers. Yet we may choose to use this knowledge to not invest. And that may be the best way to use our knowledge.

- When it seems most safe to invest is when it is not safe.

- Our enemy is not other investors. They are too busy losing money to obstruct us. We can find our enemy whenever we look in the mirror.

Let's start.

Chapter 2
Our Record

Let's face the indisputable evidence of our lack of investment skill. Remember, the goal is to learn and improve. There is a worthy cause to this unsparing self-examination.

<u>First exhibit of our extraordinary helplessness in the stock market</u>

One study found that from 1984 to 2003, the average stock fund investor earned 2.57% a year.

Let's get some context to evaluate this 2.57% a year performance.

From 1984 to 2003, a period that included the greatest stock boom in U.S. history from 1982 to 2000, the stock market returned 12.22% annually. Over 12% a year for a generation is an incredible run. But not as incredible as how investors missed this rocket ride. It is as if we were trying to fail, and we succeeded.

It gets worse.

Inflation averaged 3.14% a year from 1984 to 2003. Inflation is the increase in the price of goods (cars, groceries, phones) and services (haircuts, doctor visits, getting our house painted, piano lessons). For example, we might have noticed that the price of a typical family car increases by several hundred dollars every year. I have noticed that the price of an In-N-Out cheeseburger has increased over the years. Prices of some items, such as computers and TVs, have decreased. Overall, the price of a basket of goods and services increased by about 3% a year from 1984 to 2003. So the average stock-fund investor *lost* money after inflation.

How is it possible to lose money in stocks during the greatest stock market boom in history? At bottom, we are bad investors because we are human. Our instincts are spectacularly incompatible with profitable investing as we will see in the next chapter.

For now, let's continue to face the train wreck that is our involvement with stocks. We're not trying to be cruel. We are making sure we understand what we are up against in the market.

So, the next evidence.

<u>Second exhibit of our helplessness</u>

Let's look at another timeframe. From 1992 to 2011, the average stock investor earned about 2% a year while the overall stock market returned about 6.5% a year. And let's not forget inflation, which averaged 2.5%, again more than what the typical investor was able to earn from stocks.

Are some periods more difficult to invest in than others? Let's compare 1984 to 2003 against 1992 to 2011.

At first it may seem that the 1992 to 2011 period was the more difficult investing environment. After all, there were two historic crashes in the 1992 to 2011 period: the bursting of technology bubble of the late 1990s and the global financial crisis of 2007 to 2009. But 1992 to 2011 also had very good years. After all, it included a big chunk of the extraordinary stock boom from 1982 to 2000.

And it is not as if the 1984 to 2003 period was without scares. There was the 1987 "Black Monday" crash when stocks dropped by more than 20% in one day. There was the first Iraq war. There was the Asian financial crisis from 1997 to 1998. Also the Long-Term Capital Management crisis in 1998. And of course the technology bubble of late 1990s ensnared many people who chased hyped dotcom stocks and bought shares at the top just before the crash. And these are just some of the headline events. There were other market dips that seem inconsequential only in hindsight.

Even if we grant that some eras are "easier" to invest in than others, an immovable truth remains: *we are bad investors in all timeframes and conditions.* The period containing the largest stock market boom in history?

We did poorly. The recent era with two massive market crashes? Of course we did poorly.

The reasonable conclusion seems to be that every period has challenges. There is jarring market volatility that triggers our destructive instincts in the "gentlest" investing environments. Even when stocks go up 20% or 30% in a year, the market is fantastic at persuading people to buy at the top and sell after the slightest decline. In the next chapter we will look at the stock market in 2013 and 2014, when the market made a historic run and went up 50%, and see how millions of investors—including the highest-paid market professionals—missed the ride.

So what should we do?

It is true that had we bought low-cost index fund shares that tracked the market and "held on," we would have multiplied our money many times over from 1984 to 2003. Here's the thing though: the instruction seems simple, but it is difficult enough that few can do it. A big reason why we fail is because we are unprepared for the curveballs thrown by the market—which turns out to be an All-Galaxy pitcher with hundreds of years experience tormenting investors. Also, investment advisors and financial companies want our business, and they are more likely to get it if they don't tell us why stock investing is not so simple.

But we want to and should know. Let's see why it is so easy to lose money in stocks even when the stock market is going up and up and up. Our self-examination continues in the next chapter.

Chapter 3
Buy High and Sell Low

Let's examine the following chart:

<u>Chart 1</u>

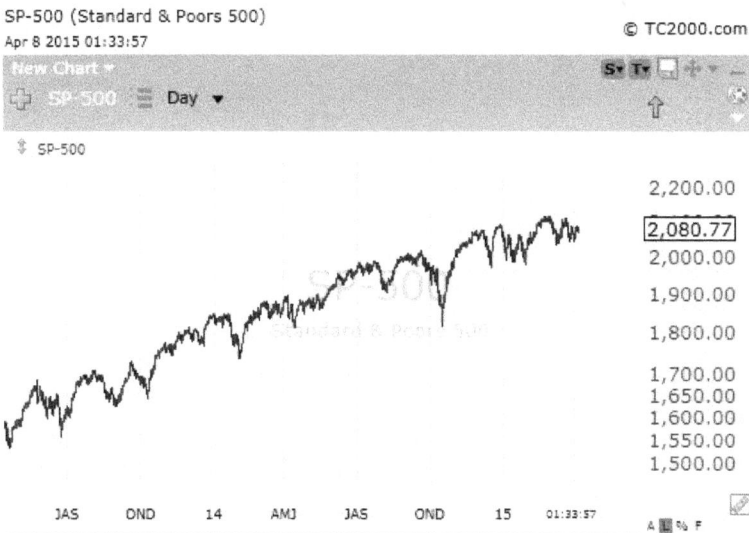

SP-500 (Standard & Poors 500)
Apr 8 2015 01:33:57

Chart 1 shows the performance of the U.S. stock market as measured by the Standard & Poor's 500 index from April 2013 to April 2015. The S&P 500 consists of 500 large companies that represent 80% of the total value of the U.S. stock market. Anybody can buy shares of a low-cost index fund that tracks the S&P 500 for less than 0.18% a year in annual expenses, which is the portion of our investment that we pay as fees to the mutual fund company.

We see a strong uptrend in Chart 1. Or, in plain English: stocks went up. To make 50%, we had to "just buy stocks and hold them." And not for

20 years, but just two years. How hard could that be? Very difficult. Our anxiety, ego, greed, and fear make sure so many of us fail an evaluation that, in some sense, tests our ability to follow the directions for boiling water.

Let's look at another chart:

Chart 2

SP-500 (Standard & Poors 500)
Apr 8 2015 01:43:43

© TC2000.com

New Chart

SP-500 Day ▼

SP-500

```
2,000.00
1,950.00
1,900.00
1,850.00
1,800.00
1,750.00
1,700.00
1,650.00
1,600.00
1,550.00
1,500.00
```

May Jun Jul Aug Sep Oct Nov Dec Jan Feb Mar 5/13/2014

Chart 2 is a close-up of Chart 1, focusing on the market from April 2013 to May 2014. 2013 was one of the best years in history for stocks as the market went up by about 32%.

How could we lose money in the stock market in 2013? Here's how: buy high and sell low. Let's look at the next chart:

Chart 3

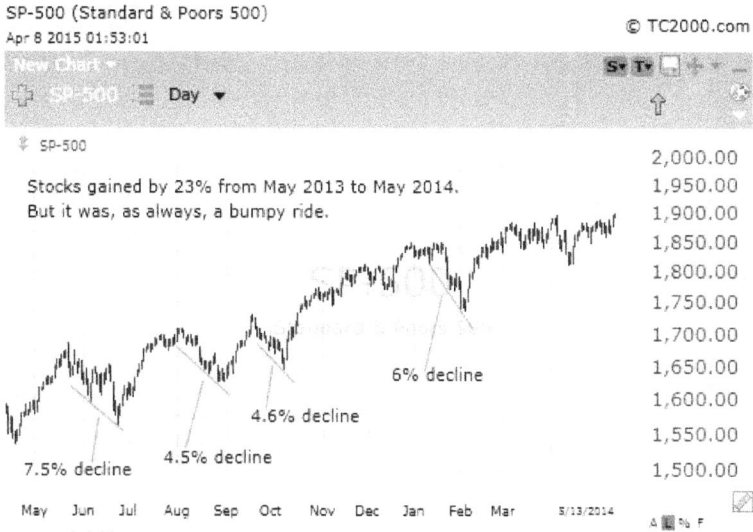

SP-500 (Standard & Poors 500)
Apr 8 2015 01:53:01
© TC2000.com

New Chart ▾   S▾ T▾ ☐ ✛ ▾ —
✛ SP-500   Day ▾   ⇧   ⊕

↕ SP-500

Stocks gained by 23% from May 2013 to May 2014.
But it was, as always, a bumpy ride.

2,000.00
1,950.00
1,900.00
1,850.00
1,800.00
1,750.00
1,700.00
1,650.00
1,600.00
1,550.00
1,500.00

6% decline
4.6% decline
7.5% decline   4.5% decline

May   Jun   Jul   Aug   Sep   Oct   Nov   Dec   Jan   Feb   Mar   5/13/2014

Chart 3 is the same as Chart 2 except that it identifies some of the many market declines that occurred within the overall uptrend from April 2013 to May 2014. These "mini" dips that seem minor in hindsight? What if we invested $30,000, $100,000, or even $5,000 when stocks were at a relative high and just before these "nothing-to-worry-about" declines? To investors who thought stocks only went up (after all, stocks return 10% every year, right?), these dips were scary events that threatened their financial future.

We are prone to start investing when stocks are going up and it finally seems "safe" to invest. But we learn that stocks can go down—a lot—even during one of the strongest bull markets in history. So we sell at the first sign of trouble because we lack conviction. And we lack conviction because we do not know what we are doing. We bought stocks because that's what our friends are doing and we heard that's how we can earn 10% a year. Sure, we expected some declines, but not so often and not so deep. Few people have the guts to hold through a 5% or 10%, let alone a 20% or 30%, decline. So we buy high and sell low.

How to buy high and sell low

Chart 4 shows the stock market's performance in 2014:

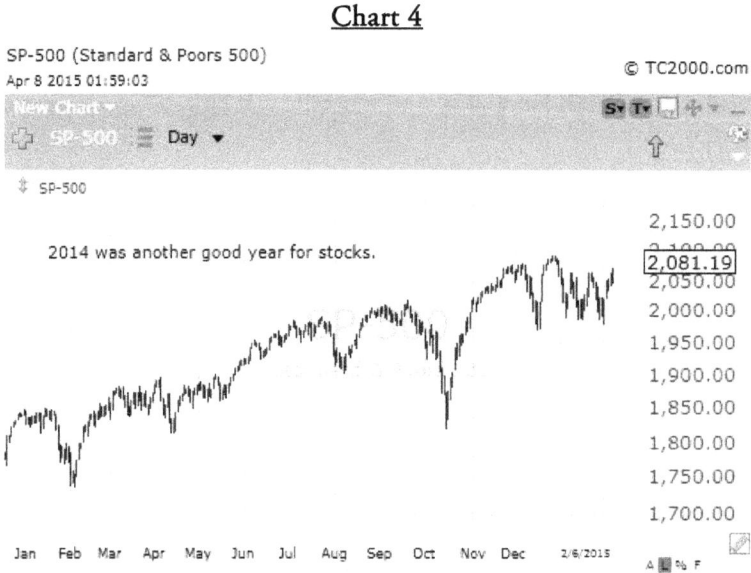

Chart 4

SP-500 (Standard & Poors 500)
Apr 8 2015 01:59:03   © TC2000.com

New Chart ▾   S▾ T▾ ⬚ ✛ ▾ ▬
⊹ SP-500 ☰ Day ▾   ⬆   ✿

⇕ SP-500

2014 was another good year for stocks.

2,150.00
2,081.19
2,050.00
2,000.00
1,950.00
1,900.00
1,850.00
1,800.00
1,750.00
1,700.00

Jan Feb Mar Apr May Jun Jul Aug Sep Oct Nov Dec   2/6/2015

The market went up by about 14% in 2014. While not as exciting as the 32% jump in 2013, we would think that it was not difficult to make money in 2014. At worst, we shouldn't have lost money, right?

Let's say we were not in stocks during the rocket-to-the-moon-ride in 2013. We were curious about—and jealous of—our friends and neighbors making money in the market. We manage to gather the courage to buy stocks, say, around the middle of September 2014. At this point the market has been going up for more than five years. It seems safe to invest. We congratulate ourselves on our patience and fine judgment. We jump into the market at the spot marked on the next chart:

Chart 5

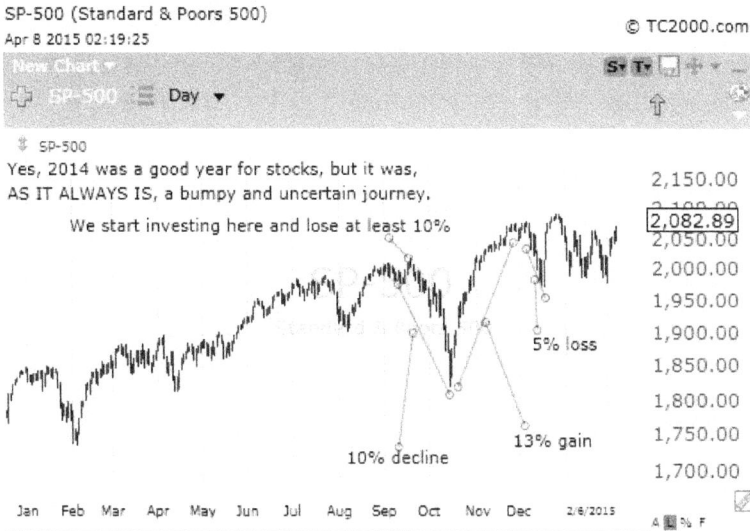

SP-500 (Standard & Poors 500)
Apr 8 2015 02:19:25

© TC2000.com

Yes, 2014 was a good year for stocks, but it was,
AS IT ALWAYS IS, a bumpy and uncertain journey.

We start investing here and lose at least 10%

2,082.89

5% loss

10% decline

13% gain

Of course when we get in, that's when the market—with delight—started a 10% decline over 30 days. In one month we were down 10% *if* we had put our money in a plain index fund. If we had bought more volatile individual stocks, then we lost 20% to 30% or more. A big chunk of our money gone. At this point, we are likely to get out with our 10% to 30% loss. We just bought high and sold low.

What if we didn't bail and held on? The market went up 13% in the next six weeks. We are up a bit. We think we figured it out. So we get greedy and put more money in stocks. Then stocks go down 5%. We get scared and sell. Buy high and sell low. Now we are down.

We are frustrated. We get more frustrated as the market goes up a quick 5% without us. So we chase and again go all in just before the next 5% drop. Now we are down quite a bit. Oh, how much worse this feels compared to being almost even just days ago. We hate the stock market. We want to get out. *And we tell ourselves that we will get out as soon as we make back our money "so that we can get out even."* As we gather our courage to go in the market again, the market jumps 3% in two days. Good, we'll catch this train and all will be well. But as soon as we get in, the market reverses and drops 3%. This tragic comedy is familiar to us. This popular drama has been showing since the beginning of markets.

If we are in this hole—and I have been—we should consider selling everything and getting out. Get out not to look for a chance to get back in but to get away from the market and stay away until we have a better sense of stocks and investing. We could take our loss and think of it as tuition for a valuable life lesson. We are bigger than our wallets. We make mistakes, and we must be mature enough to acknowledge them and learn from them. There is no need to rush into investing. The stock market will always be there if we decide to become investors after learning and reflecting. Patience. Patience. Patience.

Enough self-criticism for now. Now let's be somewhat rude and examine the record of market professionals who get paid a lot of money to pick stocks and invest our money. Surely they do better in the stock market than us?

Chapter 4
Experts Do Not Have Expertise

If you merely try
to bring just a little extra knowledge and cleverness
to ... your investment program,
instead of realizing a little better than normal results,
you may well find that you have done worse.

Benjamin Graham

We know from Chapter 3 that 2013 was a fantastic year for stocks as the market went up 32%. Surely, professionals such as mutual fund and hedge fund managers can put up at least decent performance in such a favorable year?

Out of the 30 largest hedge funds, only two performed better than the overall stock market in 2013, and only one of these two did so by a significant margin. The rest did not come close to earning 32%. More than half achieved a return of less than 15% and five funds *lost* money.

To be fair, many of these funds were in markets other than the stock market. Some investors may put a portion of their money in non-stock hedge funds so that not all of their savings are tied to the stock market. And we know that the stock market is always difficult and volatile, even in a year it gains 32%.

But is there ever a time when volatility is lacking in the markets? Isn't investing—and life—synonymous with uncertainty, change, and risk? In fact, the past couple of years have recorded some of the lowest measures of market volatility in history as the stock market marched higher. And that's key: even when stocks are going higher month after month in one of the strongest uptrends in history, it is easy for everyone—from someone who does not know the difference between a stock and a stocking to the hedge fund manager who manages billions of dollars—to lose money.

More evidence against the experts: Vanguard founder John C. Bogle points out that from 1970 to 2005, only three of 355 stock mutual funds—that's 0.8% —have a continued record of excellence. All others have lost money, lagged the market return, or gone out of business. Also, the likelihood that these three funds will continue their excellent performance for the next 35 years is tiny. And of course nobody knew in 1970 that these three funds, out of hundreds, would be the only actively-managed funds worth sticking with year after year. In short, while it is possible to beat the market over the long run, the odds of finding *and* staying with that rarer-than-rare expertise is essentially zero.

One more example of experts' lack of expertise: from 2004 to 2009, only 0.1% of fund managers specializing in picking large company stocks beat the market. Yes, there was a market crash from 2007 to 2009. But shouldn't the experts be able to do better for their clients? Shouldn't they be able to side step, at least partially, a market crash? It seems the answer is no.

So what can we do?

Part II

The "Simple Rules" For Investing: Then There Is Real Life

Chapter 5

What We Are Supposed To Do But Cannot

Over the last 60 years, the overall stock market has earned positive returns in every 20-year period. That means even if we started to invest at the top and the market crashed, we would have made money if we held on for 20 years. So we have three tasks:

1. Invest using a low-cost total stock market index fund.

2. Stay invested for 20 years or more.

3. Ignore others.

So what's so hard about following this advice? Every word. Let's see why.

Chapter 6
First Challenge: Picking the Boring Index Fund

The heart has its reasons which reason knows nothing of ....

Blaise Pascal

To make sure we have everybody on board, let's discuss what a stock index fund is.

Take the Vanguard Total Stock Market Index Fund. It tracks about 4000 stocks, almost every publicly-traded company in the U.S. The fund's annual expense ratio is 0.17%, which means that we pay Vanguard $17 a year as management fees if we invest $10,000. $17 a year is very reasonable, and it should be. After all, why should we pay a company a lot of money to manage a fund that simply follows—up and down—the stock market? Other mutual fund companies also offer a low-cost total stock market fund. If we decide to invest using an index fund, we should do our homework and make sure that the total annual expenses do not exceed 0.20% a year.

Let's revisit the facts about the choice between index funds that rise and fall with the market versus actively-managed funds run by professional stock pickers who try to beat the market. Over 20 to 30 years and longer, we can count on one hand the number of funds that will beat the market by a meaningful margin. Even if the market can be beat, a problem remains: we cannot know today which funds, whether by skill or luck, will have beaten the market 30 years later. Another problem is that many actively-managed funds don't merely fail to beat the market but give us significantly worse results than the "stupid" index fund. By going with an actively-managed fund, we pay much higher fees and take on high risk that we will do worse. There is also significant risk that we will outright lose money.

So the case for choosing a plain index fund over an actively-managed fund is compelling and logical and therefore—to humans—unpersuasive. Many of us cannot bring ourselves to invest in an index fund because it makes too much sense. Anything so rational seems cold and unrelatable. The most basic and advantageous qualities of the total stock index fund are cruel drawbacks to the optimistic and ambitious. We think there is something wrong, too passive, and even un-American about putting our money in a financial instrument that has no ambition other than to follow the market rather than try to do better. We might, just might, be okay with it when the market goes up 25% and our index fund shares are also up 25%. But even then we are likely to regret not having invested in a fund that earned 40% rather than only 25%. And it is unacceptable how our investment will sink with the market in a crash. We are individuals with unique dreams. *We cannot accept the fact that the value of our index fund shares will be so faithful to the market's ups and downs.*

We also cannot understand why all that money and brainpower on Wall Street cannot consistently beat the market. This failure contradicts our assumptions about fancy investment firms with earnest names and mottos. So we don't accept it. This denial is similar to our reaction to the record of experts at forecasting recessions and the stock market. The record is so bad—for example, the expert consensus that not a single country among the 77 being examined would be in recession in 2009 was only wrong in that forty-nine countries went into recession—that we don't believe it.

We also deny the odds we face. Remember that from 1970 to 2005, only three of 355 stock mutual funds have an excellent long-term record. We think we will be one of the few who will pick a winner. This belief leads us to ignore the much greater likelihood of doing worse than average or losing money. As Benjamin Graham noted:

A creditable, if unspectacular, result can be achieved by the [average] investor with a minimum of effort and capability …. If you merely try to bring just a little extra knowledge and cleverness to … your investment[s] …, instead of realizing a little better than normal results, you may well find that you have done worse.

I would say that striving and trying to be just a bit more clever is likely to lead to doing *much* worse. I would also say that we can achieve a spectacular result by investing in a low-cost index fund and staying invested.

But for how long?

Chapter 7
Second Challenge: Patience
(And Mind Tricks)

Genius is eternal patience.

Michelangelo

<u>Are some investors luckier than others?</u>

When we start to invest can have a big effect. For example, if we had put our entire savings in a total stock index fund around the top of the technology-stock bubble in the late 1990s, then only in 2007 did the market regain the peak it attained almost 10 years ago. Then the housing bubble burst and the stock market halved in value by early 2009. And it wasn't until early 2013 that the S&P 500 regained the level it first reached in 2000 and 2007. If we started to invest in the late 1990s and we bravely managed not to sell after two crashes, we were still essentially even 15 years later.

In contrast, investors who put in a lump sum in an index fund in the early 1980s saw the value of their investment multiply up to 10 times or more by the peak of the technology bubble of the late 1990s.

But luck in timing can be overrated. Recall that there were many setbacks even during the great bull market from 1982 to 2000. Only in hindsight do we know that these two decades were perhaps the best time to be in stocks. *We still had to possess rare determination and courage to stay*

27

invested in the market through the uncertainty that is life and investing. Life is unfair, but it is tough for all.

Spreading out our investment over time

One way to address bad timing is to spread out our purchases of index fund shares rather than making a lump sum investment. For example, Vanguard allows investors to invest as little as $25 every week or month. Investing a fixed amount on a regular basis is called dollar-cost averaging. But even with dollar-cost averaging, our challenge remains: continuing to invest *and* staying invested for the long run.

How long?

A generation

I think the minimum is at least 15 years, and really 20 to 25 years and longer. Remember that just in the past 15 years we saw two historic market crashes that each halved the value of the stock market. Also, the market has lost up to 90% of its value during a crisis such as the Great Depression of the 1930s. And yes, that can happen again.

Let's say 20 years is the minimum time. How do we stay the course 20 years? **Well-meaning supporters of index funds do not address the stiff and lifelong challenge that is staying the course for a generation.** We cannot stay the course if every time stocks decline we panic and check our investment account. Such fear, micromanagement, and futile search for reassurance will lead to meddling, chasing hot stocks and funds, going in and out of the market (buying high and selling low), and failing. Sure, we may manage to stay put for a year or even several years (perhaps—if the market is going only up, but no market does), but the true test of our staying power is when stocks go down for years.

Over any five-year or ten-year period, we will experience at least a few steep declines. In fact, we must be prepared for a 30% or more decline of our account at any time. If we don't think we can stay invested through periodic crashes, then we must not invest in stocks. There is no shame to that: it is wisdom.

Remember, investing is not easy even when stocks are surging higher. We hear about all the money being made and we rush in, all too often just before a reversal. We saw this scenario in Chapter 3.

Another scenario is when stocks go down and remain depressed. We invest after a decline and think that we are getting a better deal because we did not buy at the top of the market. But the market doesn't have to recover soon or even next year. Stocks can stay at depressed and bargain prices for years. They can even get cheaper. Then we panic and sell for a loss.

Over our 20-year timeframe, we will see all market conditions multiple times. We will see the stock market go on multi-year uptrends and downtrends at least several times. In short, staying invested for at least 20 years is an impossible feat if we are logging into our account every couple of days to check its value. So how do we avoid futile and costly meddling and worrying?

Invest and forget

Let's rephrase our mission. Instead of trying to be patient, perhaps we need to forget about our investment. That may sound irresponsible, but there isn't much to do as an index fund investor. Other than paying taxes on dividends (if we hold our index fund shares in a regular rather than tax-exempt retirement account) and completing one-time administrative tasks such as choosing beneficiaries, choosing to re-invest our dividends, and taking advantage of employer matching of 401(k) contributions if offered, there are no tasks that we must constantly attend to. *Getting one thing right—holding on—will do more good than everything else.*

Investing through an index fund means we are on auto pilot. Our investment will rise and fall with the market. Nothing we do—worry, scream, obsess, or ignore—will change the most basic feature of an index fund. We do not fight or evade or try to outsmart the market. We capture what the market gives us and nothing more, which, by the way, can multiply our investment many times over. The essential task is to do nothing as we don't have anything to think about. Of course we will think about our investment some. *The question is how to think productively to put our mind at ease as much as possible.*

<u>What are we betting on with an index fund?</u>

How might we equip our mind for the life-long journey that is investing? One way is to think about what we are counting on when we invest in an index fund. Our shares represent ownership in a slice of the U.S. economy. If the economy and American companies prosper, then this prosperity will mean higher values for our index fund shares.

Thus, we are hoping that the U.S. economy will continue to do well. What are the prospects for greater prosperity? No one can be sure, but history suggests Americans will continue to innovate and increase their wealth. Yes, there will always be challenges, such as the fact that median wages have not grown much over the last 40 years. But again and again and again, the U.S. has overcome difficulties. While past performance does not guarantee future results, I would rather bet on a dynamic country with a record of overcoming obstacles over a country that, unfortunately, has never overcome stagnation. And getting stuck at the lower- or middle-income level is the norm among countries.

<u>What if …</u>

Still, what if, though unlikely, America loses its economic preeminence over the next 30 years? Even then the chances are good that investors in U.S. companies will earn good returns. Britain lost its global economic preeminence over the 20th century, yet its stock market provided one of the highest returns in the world for long-term investors. And a more affluent world does not mean a poorer America. U.S. companies, and their investors, will benefit from a rising middle class in countries such as China and India. In any case, much more likely is America's continued global economic and political leadership.

Fine, but let's go further. Even if we do well against international competition, can we survive our own blunders? All of us at times may feel that our country's best days are past. When such gloom strikes, we should try to remind ourselves that we don't know everything, that others may have the better argument, and that things may be better than we think. And we may get some comfort from the following quote by Adam Smith:

> There is a great deal of ruin in a nation.

In other words, a country can thrive after many missteps and even tragedy and defeat. Whatever our values, at some point the dominant political and economic forces will be against our beliefs. And if we assume—a big assumption—that events and trends that are so distressing to us are objectively bad, we should still have enough humility and maturity to realize that hundreds of millions of Americans are not just sitting on their rears but instead working hard to improve their lives. A country, especially a continental power with a large population such as America, is resilient. In other words, there is a good chance that this too shall pass.

Jedi mind trick

What if things go really bad? I mean facing a disease epidemic, natural disaster, alien invasion, or some other catastrophe that threatens survival. What then of our money in the stock market? Simple: we won't care what happens to the stock market and our investment if a large asteroid hits Earth. So one way to stay invested for 20 years and more is through the following mental exercise:

> As far as these things go, America is the best bet in the world. There will be difficult times as entire industries and millions of jobs disappear due to change and competition.

But we will also create new products and services. Millions of new jobs will come from somewhere. Continued prosperity means some of the country's gains will go to investors in U.S. companies.

The best scenario is that America thrives and our investment grows many times over. The middling case is that we earn a smaller but still significant return. The worst case is that we will have less money but that won't matter because Imperial Storm Troopers will not take American dollars. *Thus, staying invested in an index fund for the long haul is the dominant strategy.*

In short, we can choose to believe—based on America's record, great human and natural resources, and some optimism (that aliens won't invade)—that things will work out. The stock market will do well if things work out okay. And stocks will be the least of our concerns if things don't work out.

<u>We assume there will be a tomorrow</u>

Is this outlook too flippant, too casual a way to think about our future? I don't think so. Every day we go about our lives assuming that we will have another chance at getting it right in the next hour, the next day, next year, and even the next decade. When we have kids, we assume that 20 to 30 years later they will have a decent opportunity to live full lives and do better than us. Our most meaningful actions—learning, loving, starting a family, helping a neighbor, and even brushing our teeth—assume that America will continue to thrive. So one might say: why not put a *portion* of our savings in an index fund under the same practical optimism that motivates us to move forward into the uncertain future? After all, the stock market has a record of incredible wealth creation—though, as we know—we don't always capture the wealth. And unlike keeping our teeth healthy, buying and holding an index fund requires no daily chore. Yes, the payoff from stocks is not guaranteed, but what is?

<u>Still, let's spread our bets</u>

Let's address another possibility. What if in 2045 the U.S. is thriving but the stock market, for whatever reason, has not rewarded long-term investors?

First, it is almost certain that over a generation or more—and especially by *reinvesting dividends*—we will at least break even or earn a modest but still meaningful return.

Second, we don't have to and shouldn't depend on the stock market doing well to secure our future. Living within our means is the most reliable and always available path to financial independence. Material things will never make for a fulfilling life. Experiences, relationships, and wisdom are far more rewarding and valuable. I know I am being annoying and preachy, but just because the talker is obnoxious does not mean the message is untrue. There is great elegance and power in living within our means, however modest our circumstances. I'm not justifying poverty or minimizing the hardships of millions of people. I am saying that if we are reading this book on a tablet computer and we have clean running water and we are bored on a Saturday afternoon because we don't know what to do, then we are better off than about 96% of humanity.

Third, diversifying can provide peace of mind against the unknowable future. And peace of mind is important. I always have a significant portion of my savings in a boring savings account even though it has paid essentially zero interest for more than six years and I am losing money after inflation. Why do something so stupid as to knowingly lose money every year? Why don't I put all of my money in the stock market if that is a win-win strategy over the next 30 years?

If it were that easy, then yes, I would invest every dime I have. But it is not that easy. Remember that it is literally a life-long challenge to stay invested for 20 or 30 years. Much detachment and an uncommon commitment to not meddle are required. Even if we "know" that the odds favor a big payoff down the road, we also know that there are no guarantees. *And it is not worth losing sleep to try to make every dollar we can.*

Our most important task as investors has nothing to do with investing

Let's return to our dilemma and potential solution. How do we stay invested for a generation? How do we "forget" about our investment? Even the most serene among us worry quite often about how our investment is doing. One way to counter unproductive worry and prevent meddling with our investment is to think the following: if we continue to innovate—and our history, resources, and advantages suggest we will—American companies will prosper and some of this prosperity will go to patient investors. This likelihood is as much certainty we can expect in investing.

Investing in the U.S. stock market for the long run is a bet on America, and that is a bet worth taking with a portion of our savings if we think we can stay invested. Meanwhile, we should focus on our family, friends, and vocation. Concentrating on living a full life rather than worrying about our investment account is—ironically—the best way to outstanding investment performance. *So then, finally, we have the essence of our task as long-term investors: living a full and meaningful life in which we don't have the time or interest to meddle with our investment for entertainment or reassurance.*

Chapter 8
Third Challenge:
Ignoring Others

The investment business is a giant scam.

Jack Meyer, former manager of Harvard's endowment

By accepting one fact—that a low-cost index fund that tracks the overall market does better than essentially all other attempts to make money in the stock market—we are way ahead. By acting on this truth and staying the course with an index fund for the next 20 years or more, we will likely do better than 99% of all investors.

Then why do we not see every investment firm and advisor urge people to become long-term investors in an efficient index fund?

<u>Self-interest</u>

Wider use of low-cost index funds is not in the interest of the financial services industry. Remember that anyone can invest in a total market index fund for less than 0.18% a year in expenses. Compare this tiny expense to the cost of actively-managed funds (funds that—futilely—try to beat the market by picking stocks) that charge 1% to 2% or more every year. Investment firms make much more selling these aspirational—and pointless and likely harmful—products, so they tend not to emphasize the quiet and unbeatable advantages of index funds. Saving 1% or more a year in fees over 30 years can mean hundreds of thousands or even millions of dollars more for us rather than Wall Street.

It's our fault

We can't blame everything on Wall Street. As noted, many of us cannot accept tying ourselves to an index fund and getting dragged down by every market decline. We want to be nimble and in control. We want to take more than what the market gives us.

The financial services industry knows our psychology. It knows our ambition and impatience. It knows our yearning to know the future. It knows we want to be associated with fancy—and expensive—investment strategies. It knows we like confident and entertaining forecasts. So it gives us what we want.

Is there any justification to choose a mutual fund that charges us 1.5% to 2% a year over the thrifty index fund that asks for only 0.18%? Do we get anything out of the costlier product? Sure, we get the thrill—short-lived—of buying a service that aspires like we do. If we are choosing this route, then we should do so knowing the facts. And we know the facts. Over 20 years or more, which is our timeline, essentially no actively-managed fund beats the market. And we cannot know today which two or three or maybe five or six—out of thousands—will do so 30 years later. And many funds will lag the market return or lose money outright.

Investing and fast food

Still, we are stubborn. Could so much of what an industry sells be so counter-productive?

I don't think everything about Wall Street is bad. There are excellent choices in the investing world, perhaps the best being the low-cost total stock market fund. We have to be informed consumers to make the right choices.

In this sense I think Wall Street is like fast food. Fast food is convenient and sometimes delicious. And—if we choose well—it can even be healthy. An occasional greasy high-calorie meal at a favorite spot is okay if the rest of our meals are healthy. For me, nothing brings back childhood memories like a Chicken McNugget, and I enjoy occasionally eating McNuggets even if it contains ingredients I cannot pronounce (such as Dimenthylpolysiloxane). I love eating a cheeseburger and fries with a vanilla shake at In-N-Out every now and then as well. With self-discipline we can splurge sometimes, which seems to be the meaning behind the saying "everything in moderation, including moderation."

So maybe another way to get ourselves to choose and stay with an index fund—the investing equivalent of a diet of mostly fruits and vegetables—is to budget for and enjoy an occasional triple cheeseburger in our investment diet. One approach might be to put in at least 90% of the portion of our savings meant for investment in a humble total market index fund while using the rest for more adventurous—and riskier—bets. We might put some of the adventure money in a well-regarded actively-managed stock fund that charges no more than about 0.5% to 0.6% a year in expenses. If we want to get really involved in the market, then we might even pick or trade stocks on our own (of course with only a very small portion of our savings). We'll talk about these alternative—and never forget, riskier—approaches to the stock market next in Part III.

Isaac Newton was smart — and human

Before moving on, here's a story: Isaac Newton lost a fortune during the great speculative bubble in the South Sea Company. Newton bought shares early and sold for a profit. Then, in the searing words of investment manager Jeremy Grantham, the worst thing that could happen to an investor happened to Newton: *he saw his friends get rich.* South Sea Company shares went up 1000%.

There is humor here. There are also uncomfortable truths about human nature: truths that no one is immune from. At times, we are all greedy. We can lose our values when money is involved. And when friends are involved—and especially when friends are making a lot of money (friends, according to our humble judgment, who are not smarter than us)—that is a moment of danger. It seems Newton reacquired South Sea shares near the peak of the bubble and lost a fortune when the mania crashed.

This story points to *an underappreciated truth: emotional control is more important than intelligence in keeping us away from fads and manias*. Even if we avoid financial bubbles and penny stocks, many of us will want to explore stocks on our own. So next we'll talk about how we might safely direct our energies and curiosity.

Part III

Other Approaches
to the Stock Market

Chapter 9
Picking Stocks

What are the prospects of [picking individual stocks that will be] more profitable than [an index fund]? We would be less than frank … if we did not at the outset express some grave reservations on this score.

&

We are thus led to the following logical if disconcerting conclusion: To enjoy a reasonable chance for continued better than average results, the investor must follow policies that are (1) inherently sound and promising, and (2) not popular on Wall Street.

Benjamin Graham

In this chapter we will discuss how we might go about picking stocks using the principles in Benjamin Graham's *The Intelligent Investor.* Understanding just a few of Graham's straightforward concepts will make us better investors.

Before we jump in, here's an amazing thing about Graham: the person who laid out perhaps the most logical, rational, and intelligent way to analyze stocks asked whether we should pick stocks at all given the significant possibility—perhaps likelihood—that it may be a futile and costly endeavor. If Graham the master investor had such caution and awareness, then we must also.

<u>Graham's investment approach</u>

We'll discuss two of Graham's methods:

#1: Consider a stock selling at a price lower than the company's net current assets.

Please do not worry if you have never heard of net current assets. We will learn this simple and powerful concept together.

#2: Consider a stock selling not far above its book value.

Again, do not worry. We will easily grasp book value as well.

Net-current-asset value and book value are two ways of calculating a company's liquidation value: the value of assets remaining for shareholder-investors after paying all debts. The idea is that if we buy shares at a price around the stock's net-current-asset value or book value, then we have a good chance of recovering a significant portion, if not all, of our investment even if the company goes bankrupt. Such an emphasis on *investment safety* helps us avoid dangerous stocks and evaluate attractive investment opportunities.

<u>First investment method: consider a stock selling at less than the company's net current assets</u>

Under the "net current assets" approach to a potential stock pick, we go to a company's *balance sheet*. The balance sheet tells us a company's financial health by telling us the value of the things it owns (assets) and its debts (liabilities). All publicly-traded companies (companies whose shares we can buy and sell through our stock broker) must file financial statements, including its balance sheet, every three months.

Let's look at a real balance sheet. Below is a portion of a recent balance sheet of Chipotle Mexican Grill (stock symbol CMG), where I've had many burritos over the years. Just relax and follow along. We can find this information online for free. We can go to the company's website and look up the 10-Q or 10-K filing in the Investor Relations section. Or we can go to sites such as Yahoo Finance or Google Finance and type in CMG in the search box. Let's look at Chipotle's Current Assets:

Current Assets = $879 million as of December 31, 2014, which includes:

— Cash

— Other things that can be converted easily into cash (such as short-term government bonds)

— Receivables (cash that Chipotle can collect from customers and businesses)

— Inventory (things like tortillas, avocadoes, tomatoes, meat, and beans that Chipotle has in its stores and warehouses)

"Current" assets are cash and other things that can be immediately or at least relatively easily converted into cash. Current assets do not include more long-term assets like factories, heavy equipment like grills, and real estate, which are listed separately. While things like land and cooking equipment are valuable, their value is not as fixed as cash in the bank and not as easily converted into cash. For example, the land Chipotle owns is valuable, but it can take weeks, months, and even years to sell real estate. Also, land prices fluctuate a lot. Land that we bought for $1 million three years ago may be worth only $500,000 in a recession. Or take the grill in our restaurants. Let's say we bought each grill for $30,000. I'm sure someone is willing to buy our grills, but at what price? They were custom made for Chipotle and thus may not fit other kitchens. Thus, someone may buy them only at a steep discount. So the price at which we might sell our land, grills, and other long-term property is uncertain. Including them in our tally of a company's value could inflate the company's finances. The idea is to be as conservative as possible in valuing a company to maximize our chances of losing as little money as possible even if a company goes bankrupt.

Now let's look at how much Chipotle owes to banks, suppliers, and others, which is found in the "Liabilities" section, just below "Assets":

> **Total Liabilities** = $534 million.

Hang in there for another 30 seconds.

To calculate "net current assets," we subtract the total amount Chipotle owes, $534 million, from its cash and almost-cash pile, $879 million:

> $879 million *minus* $534 million = $345 million of **net current assets**.

Graham advised us to consider investing in a stock selling at a price lower than the company's "net current assets." With this approach, Graham is asking us to adopt the mindset of a rational business person when analyzing a stock. Let's see how.

Consider: let's say we own Chipotle. We know that our company has $345 million in net current assets. *That is $345 million left over after paying all debts. And* this $345 million does *not* include other long-term assets such as the land (stores) and equipment (grills). It also does not include the value of the Chipotle brand and customer goodwill.

Now a question: would we sell Chipotle—the entire company—for $300 million?

Of course not.

Why would we give away our company for $300 million when the company has $345 million in the bank after paying all debts, not counting all that valuable other stuff? And of course there is also the underlying business that serves millions of customers every week. A sale price of $300 million values Chipotle's business at *minus* $45 million. That's right, not $1, $1 million, $1 billion, or $10 billion—but negative $45 million. Now, there are instances when a business has negative value due to things like legal liabilities, pending lawsuits, regulatory issues, and large debts. Assuming Chipotle has no legal problems and is in good financial shape, its owners would never sell Chipotle for $300 million when the company has $345 million in cash alone after paying back all debt and not counting the fabulous underlying business and other property.

Another question: would we buy Chipotle if we had the cash and chance to buy the company for $300 million?

Of course. But what irrational owner would sell at a price less than the value of the cash in the bank after paying all debts?

Well, throughout the stock market's history—though rarer today—such fascinating opportunities are found, especially during economic downturns. Yet time and time again almost everyone refused to consider investing in such companies. Why?

Because most people had spent their financial and emotional capital chasing trendy stocks before the crash.

Because most "investors" do not know the basics of a balance sheet and wouldn't know the significance of a company with good prospects selling for a price below the amount of cash it has clear of all debt.

Because people do not bring a business mindset to stocks.

Such a bizarrely golden opportunity tends to arise during deep economic downturns when one must have the cash and courage to invest. That said, when—not if—the next economic crisis strikes, similar opportunities are likely to arise again.

It is important to note that studying the balance sheet is just one step. Even if a company is selling for less than or around its net-current-asset value, it must also have good prospects, honest and skilled management, and a stable earnings history to be an attractive investment. And stocks that meet these criteria were more common during Graham's day. That said, we shouldn't look down on the net-current-asset value approach as our grandparents' way of doing things that we have no use for. After all, the approach has a beneficial and rational logic to it, which is something we cannot say about our own "investing methods." And the logic is this: if we buy a stock at around its net current asset value, then we have a good chance of recovering some or even most of our money even if the company were to fail. How? Because net current assets are the cash we have after deducting all debt and paying off banks and bondholders. Absent surprises such as legal liabilities or accounting fraud, the remaining cash is for shareholders.

Still, nothing is guaranteed in investing except risk. It is possible to lose money investing in a company selling below its leftover cash after paying all debt. So we should not put all our money in one or even several stocks, no matter how attractive they seem. Beginners should be especially careful. As noted, there are often good reasons—accounting irregularities or fraud, potentially massive legal liabilities, etc.—why a stock is priced so low. So we must diversify. If we think we found a genuine bargain stock with good prospects and record of consistent profitability, we must still be cautious and put in no more than a small portion of that part of our savings meant for investment—assuming we have decided, after careful thought, to pick stocks on our own.

Quick recap

Let's pause and review.

First, we learned how to read a company's balance sheet.

Second, we learned one rational and logical way we might evaluate a stock: the net-current-asset approach. If a stock is selling below or near the amount of the company's cash pile *after deducting all debt*—and the underlying business has good prospects and a solid record—then we might consider investing in the stock. The net-current-asset approach is about minimizing our chances of losing money by investing in stocks with a built-in margin of safety. After all, nobody knows the future. So Graham recommended investment techniques such as the net-current-asset approach that that *relied as little as possible on being right about a company's future.* Instead, he focused on a solid foundation today based on, among other things, cash in the bank. We'll talk about the enticement—and risk—of investing based on optimistic company forecasts when we discuss Graham's second investing method.

<u>Should we invest in Chipotle under the net-current-asset analysis?</u>

Before moving on to Graham's second strategy, let's discuss whether we should invest in Chipotle based on the net-current-asset approach. I type in Chipotle's symbol, CMG, at the Yahoo Finance site. I scroll down and click on "Balance Sheet" on the left side of the screen. I calculate Chipotle's net current assets, which we found was $345 million. Then I click on "Key Statistics," which is also on the left side of the page. Under the Valuation Measures section, the first entry is Market Cap, as in Market Capitalization or the total value of the company in the stock market. The total market value of Chipotle was $20.6 billion on March 27, 2015.

Chipotle is selling far above the company's net-current-asset value and thus doesn't qualify for investment consideration, at least under the net-current-asset approach. We realize the strictness and uncompromising safety-first purpose of Graham's net-current-asset test. It is a very conservative approach. A business such as Chipotle will not be on sale at a price anywhere near its cash stash alone unless the economy is in a deep recession and there are doubts about Chipotle's future. But just because an approach does not immediately produce an investment idea does not mean the approach is wrong. *The important thing is that Graham's net-current-asset approach gives us a logical and business-minded way to think about investing.*

<u>Second investment method: consider a stock selling not far above its book value.</u>

Let's go back to Chipotle's balance sheet and learn how to calculate *book value*. Again, don't worry and just follow along.

First, let's figure out a company's "shareholder equity." Actually, we don't have to figure it out because it is done for us but it is good to know how we could do it ourselves: we take all our assets and subtract from it all our debts.

Chipotle's total assets—both current assets and others—are $2.55 billion. Chipotle's total debts (same thing as total liabilities) are $534 million.

So:

> $2.55 billion *minus* $534 million = approximately $2 billion in shareholder equity.

We'll see that all of this is done for us when using a site such as Yahoo Finance. When we pull up Chipotle's Balance Sheet, we see that the second from the last entry at the bottom shows:

Total Stockholder Equity: $2.012 billion

From here, we do one more thing to calculate book value: we subtract from $2 billion the amount of "intangible assets" that Chipotle owns. Chipotle has $21 million of intangible assets. We subtract $21 million from Total Stockholder Equity of just over $2 billion and we get a Book Value of still around $2 billion. Intangible assets include trademarks, patents, and goodwill. The thinking behind subtracting intangible assets is that while they are often valuable, their value can be too imprecise and therefore including them could inflate and distort a company's financial condition. Although not as strict as the net-current-assets approach since book value includes long-term assets like real estate, factories, and cooking equipment in addition to cash, book value is still a conservative tally of a company's worth. Remember, *the less generous we are in measuring a company's worth, the more difficult it will be for the company to pass our tests of investment safety.* The point is to eliminate most stocks from investment consideration until a few truly attractive candidates are left.

By the way, book value is also calculated for us. The last line in the Balance Sheet for Chipotle in Yahoo Finance is "Net Tangible Assets," which is another name for Book Value.

What's backing up our investment?

Now that we figured out Chipotle's book value, let's see what it tells us about investing in Chipotle shares. Graham's second investment approach was to consider investing in a company selling not far above its book value. Here is Graham:

> Investments made at or below 133% of book value may *with logic be regarded as related to the company's balance sheet* and as *having support independent of fluctuating market prices.* (emphasis added)

This line is one my favorite parts from *The Intelligent Investor.*

First, Graham gives us a specific number: consider investing in a stock selling at no more than 33% above the company's book value.

Second, Graham asks us: *wouldn't it be nice to have some tangible basis, some hard assets such as cash, land, factories, and inventory—some collateral—backing up our investment?* Graham is urging us to treat stock investing as we would any business endeavor. Consider: no responsible bank would loan us money unless we have some asset that the bank can take if we fail to repay the loan. Yet we seem to forget that we risk our money when we buy shares. In fact, buying shares is more risky than lending money to a company because shareholders are last in line to be distributed—if anything is left—a company's assets should the company go bankrupt.

Back to Chipotle. Chipotle was valued at about $20.5 billion in March 2015 when its book value was only $2 billion. Its share price was $662.72 and its book value per share was only about $65 a share. So the company was valued at 10 times its book value. Buying one share of Chipotle stock for $660 means only $65 of our investment was backed by real "stuff" (cash, property, equipment, etc.) that Chipotle owned. So what's the extra $600 for? For what reason and payoff would a person risk an additional $600?

<u>Are we buying value or hype?</u>

This $600 gap is where stock picking becomes tricky and risky. Let's examine some arguments in favor of investing in Chipotle at over $600 a share. The following is what current investors in Chipotle might say:

> Yes, Chipotle shares are expensive if you consider only its book value, which is cash and physical assets. But book value is a stagnant measure as it is about how much money has been invested into the company and how much stuff a company has. We are interested in how efficiently Chipotle makes money using its assets. Other fast-casual restaurants can have the same grills and chairs and even menu as Chipotle, but competitors lack Chipotle's food quality, customer service, branding, and overall execution. Management skill, employee training, and strategy matter. And Chipotle has these things plus a unique story based on healthier and more ethical ingredients.

> We are especially excited about Chipotle's *future* growth and earnings. While Chipotle's stock price is far above the company's book value, if Chipotle's sales and profits

continue to grow at a fast rate—and we think they will—today's share price is a good deal and perhaps even a bargain.

These are reasonable points. How well a company uses its assets—and not just how much stuff it has—can make all the difference. Two ice cream shops can have the same high-quality ice cream and equipment but one store may offer superior service and ambience and thus enjoy higher sales and profits. The store with the better business execution is more valuable. *The question, though, is whether the forecast—never a guarantee—of continued success justifies paying such a high premium over a company's book value.*

Let's say that Chipotle's current stock price assumes a 10% growth rate for the next 10 years. If the company beats expectations and grows by 15% every year, then Chipotle's stock is likely—though never guaranteed—to reward people who bought Chipotle at over $600 a share. And it is easy to believe in a bright future for Chipotle. Many have embraced Chipotle's higher-quality ingredients, story, and value proposition. When I'm on the road and looking for a filling and relatively healthy meal at a good price, I look for a Chipotle.

But would I buy Chipotle shares at over $600?

My opinion is no. Here's why. Remember that we assumed that Chipotle's stock price already reflects a 10% growth rate. For the stock to go higher, it must at least match or do better than expectations. Chipotle may grow at 15% or even 20% a year. *But it may not.* Chipotle could be a trendsetting and historic success even if it grew at only 7% a year. But several percentage points make a huge difference for the stock price. If Chipotle grows at 7% a year for the next 10 years, then it could still be a business success but it likely will not reward people who bought its stock at $660 a share on the hope that Chipotle would grow at 10% or more. Indeed, there is a significant chance that these investors will lose a lot of money. Almost everything must go right for Chipotle to achieve or surpass investors' high expectations.

But life is uncertain. Consumer tastes change and new trends and competitors emerge. And so the company may grow at only 7% a year. As investors realize Chipotle's growth has slowed, they may value Chipotle at only $300 a share. Chipotle is still a good company. It may be the most admired restaurant chain in America. But none of that prevents people who bought Chipotle at $660 a share from losing half of their money.

So the risk in buying Chipotle at $660 a share is the significant possibility that Chipotle will fail to grow as rapidly as people forecast. Graham's repeated warning against investing in trendy "growth" stocks stems from the fact that all too often hot stocks fail to live up to great expectations and their stock prices collapse. And even if expectations are met or even surpassed, investors' euphoric optimism may mean that the stock price today already reflects the highest growth rate Chipotle could achieve. And so the stock can only go down.

<u>We can wait</u>

Let's say we decided that Chipotle, despite its current success and promising future, was too expensive and risky an investment at its current stock price. So we pass on Chipotle for now.

Assume that five years later the economy is in recession and the stock market has declined by 35%. Let's also say that the price of Chipotle shares have declined by over 70% in our hypothetical world. Chipotle's sales growth and profits have declined because the competition is catching up. Traditional fast-food names such as McDonald's are offering healthier items at lower prices. Chipotle is also facing rising costs as it tries to secure higher-quality ingredients. And people are eating out less in a tough economy.

We remember how we wanted to buy Chipotle shares five years ago but decided they were too expensive. Perhaps now is a better time. So we look into the company. We conclude—after careful investigation—that Chipotle is still growing (although not as quickly as people hoped it would), gets high marks from customers, and has a loyal and growing following. It continues to make a profit in a tough economy. We also know that the economy will get better and people will enjoy eating out more with their family and friends as their personal finances improve.

Then we look at Chipotle's financials. Let's say that its balance sheet shows a book value of $5 billion. After a 70% decline in the stock price, Chipotle's total market value has declined from $20 billion to $6 billion. Let's say that these numbers work out to a $200 per share stock price and a $170 per share book value.

Compare these numbers from five years ago: then, Chipotle's book value was $2 billion (or $65 a share) and its total market value was over $20 billion (or $660 a share). Five years ago people valued Chipotle at $18 billion over book value and paid $600 over book value for each share based on the forecast and hope that Chipotle would continue to grow at a certain pace. When Chipotle grew slower than hoped for and the economy went into recession, its stock price crashed.

Now things get interesting. In our judgment, Chipotle has good prospects. The company continues to make money even in a deep recession and is still growing. Of course we could be wrong about Chipotle's prospects, just as people who bought Chipotle at $660 a share five years ago were wrong about how fast Chipotle would grow.

But consider: *were we to invest in Chipotle at $200 a share, about $170 of our $200 investment would be backed by the cash and tangible assets that Chipotle owns.* In a sense, only $30 of our money would be subject to the whims and fantasies of fickle shareholders and the market. Let's recall Graham:

> A stock investment made not too far above a company's book value "may with logic be regarded as related to the company's balance sheet and as having support independent of fluctuating market prices."

If we invest in Chipotle at $200 a share—not too far above Chipotle's book value of $170 a share—"we can take a much more independent and detached view of stock-market fluctuations than those who have paid high multiples of both earnings and book value." By the way, we will discuss the earnings multiple in Chapter 13.

So investors who buy Chipotle at $200 a share with $170 of tangible book value behind them along with good business prospects and continued profitability have much more than hope to stand on through the market's gyrations and life's uncertainties. For these investors, if the stock price declines to $150 a share or even lower amid increasing market panic, they can still have confidence in their investment as long as Chipotle maintains a strong financial position and continues to have good prospects. *In fact, they might buy more shares.* These investors know that cash and hard assets, in addition to good prospects and profitability, stand behind their investment *no matter what panicking investors and the fluctuating market say.*

Meanwhile, many who bought Chipotle at $660 a share will sell at $200 a share. This unfortunate scenario plays out again and again. Graham devoted a couple of chapters in *The Intelligence Investor* to instances when people bought trendy stocks at stunningly expensive prices and ignored solid companies with good prospects whose shares were selling below or near book value. These people sold their growth stocks for crushing losses when the hype disappeared, as it always does.

Our tasks

Intelligent investing means we do not invest in a stock because we like the company's product or because we have a "hunch" or because the media is talking about the company. It requires analyzing a company's balance sheet, earnings history, and prospects. It also requires, as we will learn in Chapter 13, consideration of how expensive the stock is in relation to the company's earnings. And most of all, intelligent investing requires patience. Good companies with promising futures are often not attractive investments because high expectations and investor enthusiasm have made the stock expensive. However, periodically—whether because of a stumble or a recession—quality companies sell for an attractive price. Until the right time, intelligent investors wait and do their homework. If we find such patience and objective analysis unappealing, then we should not be picking individual stocks.

And we must not underestimate the patience required. Waiting for an attractive investment opportunity means that we may watch from the sidelines for many years as an expensive stock market becomes more expensive, more exciting, and more dangerous. In 1965, Graham said that he had "no enthusiasm for common stocks at [current market] levels ...." He repeated these words in 1972.

Even after much patience, we still have to choose wisely. Most stocks get crushed during a recession. But we cannot just pick any depressed stock. As we know, there are often good reasons why a stock is selling below or near book value or net-current-asset value. While many businesses and their share prices recover with the economy, not all companies survive a recession. Even if they survive, companies may never regain their former position. Times change. Managers make mistakes. Competitors steal customers. New technologies make entire industries obsolete.

So a good balance sheet is not enough. Shrinking business opportunities mean the large pile of cash can disappear in months. Graham tells us that we must diversify by finding at least a dozen or so stocks that have good prospects, low debt, and a reasonable earnings multiple (which we'll discuss in Chapter 13). And it is not easy to appraise the prospects of a company in a dynamic global economy.

Then we must hold our investment through the ups and downs of the market.

After all this, the end result may be the same as or worse than investing in a humble index fund. Thus Graham's saying: "If you merely try to bring just a little extra knowledge and cleverness to ... your investment program, instead of realizing a little better than normal results, you may well find that you have done worse."

Making allowances for our fallibility

As we noted, some investors emphasize the profits a company is *projected* to earn. They calculate the present value of a company's future stream of income and compare it to today's stock price. So, they argue that even if Chipotle's book value does not support the stock price, the present value of Chipotle's *estimated* future profits justifies investing in Chipotle today at $660 a share.

But no matter how elegant and sophisticated the math used to calculate the present value of Chipotle's expected income, that formula must be fed someone's very unscientific guess about Chipotle's future profits. After all, forecasts are mere speculations. The calculated present value is only as accurate as the forecast. Or, more crudely: garbage in, garbage out.

Graham warned about the seductive pull of claimed mathematical precision in investing, a game without any certainty:

> In 44 years of Wall Street experience and study, I have *never seen dependable calculations made about common-stock values*, or investment policies, *that went beyond simple arithmetic* or the most elementary algebra. Whenever calculus is brought in, or higher algebra, you could take it as a *warning signal* that the [person] was trying to substitute theory for experience, and usually also to *give to speculation the deceptive guise of investment.* (emphasis added)

Recall that we used nothing more than addition and subtraction to calculate Chipotle's book value and net-current-asset value. Of course book value is far from the perfect investment tool. We know that book value is just one of several factors the intelligent investor considers. And an estimate of the future *is* part of the consideration. After all, the stock picker must analyze a company prospects. We cannot avoid doing some forecasting. The point is that we should not mostly or even significantly base our investment on an optimistic forecast. By requiring a stock meet demanding requirements such as a long record of good earnings and a stock price close to book value, we can be wrong—by quite a bit—about the future and still make money or at least not lose too much money. Stock pickers, Graham said, should demand such a "margin of safety" in their investments.

Has investing changed from Graham's day?

Some make a more fundamental objection to Graham: because returns on capital today are higher than in Graham's day, most stocks trade well above book value and analyzing the balance sheet does not tell us much about whether a stock is overpriced or a bargain. If so, then what other clear and logical method can we use to analyze stocks? Some of the best investors to follow Graham's teachings are not sure there is a better method. Here are the authors of *Value Investing: From Graham to Buffett and Beyond*:

> [I]n practice the investment strategy of buying shares selling in the market for a *significant discount to book value* has proved *difficult to improve upon.* (emphasis added)

So we are back to the "old" wisdom of Graham. As we will see in Chapter 12, stocks today (as of April 2015) are very expensive according to some measures. There will be fewer stocks that pass Graham's strict tests of investment safety in a pricey market. Just because emphasizing safety and financial conservatism reveal less investment candidates than before does not mean caution is bad. *Instead, we should be even more cautious and patient.* The last thing we should do is conclude that we can do whatever we want and take more risks. The better approach is to wait for those occasions when Graham's insights are applicable. We may wait a while, but when the time comes, we will know that we are using an understandable and rational method to invest. Until then, doing nothing may be best. Nobody forces us to be in the market.

Conclusion

Some may be disappointed that *The Intelligent Investor* emphasizes what not to do and how to eliminate risky stocks from investment consideration rather than how to always be in stocks. It stresses patience, logic, and independence to first and foremost prevent losses. It is not about quick profits. Of course we know there is no way to get rich quickly in stocks or anywhere else, right?

Then we should realize that eliminating risky stocks from consideration is perhaps the most valuable way to apply our new knowledge. There will always be more chances to make money. But it is difficult to recover if we gamble and lose on a stock that we never would have invested in had we applied Graham's principles. We must remember what the financial historian and investment analyst Peter L. Bernstein said: "Survival is the only road to riches." Before we become successful investors, we must first protect our savings by adopting a safety-first mindset.

For example, doing nothing and leaving our money in a savings account paying no interest is far better than chasing a trendy stock and making money. That's right—it is worse to make money taking an irresponsible risk than to stuff our money in our mattress because we learn all the wrong lessons from that profitable gamble. We become emboldened and continue to take big risks. But our luck will run out.

If we decide to pick stocks on our own, we *will* meet disaster if we forget Graham's lessons. Only if we can tolerate the loneliness that comes with independent thinking, only if we refuse to participate in the market's euphoric fantasies, only if we work to continuously remind ourselves of Graham's timeless truths, and only if we have the courage to keep our minds open when others are panicking during dark economic times, only then do we have a chance of earning good and perhaps market-beating returns by investing in individual stocks.

Chapter 10
Trading Stocks

There is intelligent speculation as there is intelligent investing ….

Benjamin Graham

So few succeed in the market because people want to get rich quickly.

Jesse Livermore

If we are going to speculate in stocks—and we must never forget that trading stocks is speculating—we should do so responsibly and intelligently. Only when we master responsible trading can we make money.

Many would say that not speculating is the only intelligent trading there is. I have much sympathy for this sentiment. But even if we choose and stick with an index fund, many of us will also trade stocks or at least be curious about it. So this chapter is for those who think they might be interested in learning how to trade stocks. It provides a concise overview of one approach to trading. This chapter is at most a first step for future stock traders.

Another warning: we must never speculate with money that we cannot afford to lose. If we decide to trade stocks, we should do so using only a small portion of our savings: an amount the loss of which will not affect our family obligations and financial security. Trading has a long and steep learning curve. We will lose money in the learning process. And learning the market takes time. I agree with those who say that it takes a couple of years to learn how to maneuver in the market and several more years to be ready to start consistently making money, if we are still standing. Even then big losses are never far away if traders fail to follow strict risk management. Profitable trading can be done, but we will find it one of the most difficult tasks we have undertaken. The difficulty is not so much in learning the trading principles but following them. Traders find that their emotions push them away from good trading practices.

Requirements for intelligent speculation

Intelligent speculation is making bets only on those occasions when the *possible* gains are much greater than the *likely* losses. It stresses limiting losses and protecting our trading capital rather than making money. It allows a trader to have more losing than winning trades and yet still be profitable overall through strict money management.

How do we spot set-ups with a favorable reward-to-risk possibility? We'll use classical charting principles to illustrate this concept. Classical charting is about trading geometric patterns (rectangles, triangles, etc.) that form in stock prices. I find classical charting so useful and fascinating that I wrote a book about it: *Trading Stocks Using Classical Chart Patterns: A Complete Tactical and Psychological Guide for Beginners and Experienced Traders*. If you find interesting the following introduction to classical charting, you may want to consider the book as a resource. There are countless trading systems. We are free to choose the method that fits our personality and style. I use classical charting as a trader because it is a versatile approach that allows for uncompromising risk control. Whichever trading method we choose, the most important things are that the approach allows us to strictly manage our risk *and that we do so*.

Spotting a favorable set-up and limiting risk

Let's look at the following chart:

Chart 6

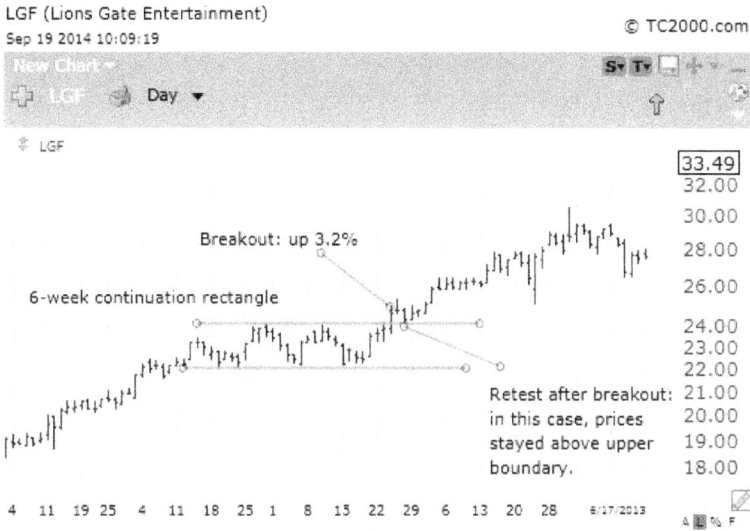

LGF (Lions Gate Entertainment)
Sep 19 2014 10:09:19

© TC2000.com

New Chart ▾

LGF 🐷 Day ▾

LGF

33.49
32.00
30.00
28.00
26.00
24.00
23.00
22.00
21.00
20.00
19.00
18.00

Breakout: up 3.2%

6-week continuation rectangle

Retest after breakout:
in this case, prices
stayed above upper
boundary.

4 11 19 25 4 11 18 25 1   8   15 22 29 6   13 20 28   6/17/2013

Chart 6 is Lions Gate Entertainment's stock chart from February to June 2013. Note how the stock went from $19 a share in early February to around $23 a share by the middle of March. Then shares traded for 7 weeks within a narrow price range between $22 and $24 and formed a rectangle pattern before breaking out of the rectangle and continuing higher to $30 a share a month later.

A classical chart trader may decide to buy shares on the day when the stock price went up 3.2% and closed above the upper boundary of the rectangle as indicated on Chart 6. Let's say we buy 100 shares at around $25 a share, near the stock's closing price on the breakout day. Then we *must* place a stop-loss order in our brokerage account that will automatically sell our 100 shares and cut our losses if the stock price reverses and comes back inside the rectangle instead of going higher. So we place a stop-loss order at, say, $23.65, which is just below the breakout day's low price (low price is the lowest price at which the stock traded that day). The rationale for placing our stop here is that if the breakout from the rectangle has significance, then our stop has a reasonable chance of not getting triggered by normal price swings. However, there are zero guarantees in stock trading. The stock price can decline and barely trigger our stop and then turn around and shoot higher. If this scenario happens then we must not get angry and chase the stock. We must remain composed and remember that there will be other opportunities. If our stop is triggered, we would lose about $150 including trading commissions. A classical chart trader may decide that this risk is worth taking given the well-defined rectangle pattern and a favorable entry spot that limits our possible loss.

In this case, prices returned to the upper boundary two days after the breakout. Such a "retest" of the breakout boundary is common. Sometimes the boundary fails to hold and prices return inside the pattern and trigger our stop. Here, the boundary held and prices went higher. We sell our shares a month later at around $29 a share and make a profit of around $500. Chart traders are not long-term investors. We may hold the stock from as short as a few days to perhaps several weeks or months depending on various factors. Note that we didn't analyze a stock's book value, prospects, or earnings history. Many chart traders analyze solely the price to trade.

This trade was profitable and ideal. But not all trades will be so pleasant and straightforward. We must learn to deal with the frustration, anger, resentment, regret, and greed that trading provokes. Remember, this chapter is just a brief look at one approach to trading stocks. And to stress the fact that trading is a risky endeavor that will challenge us to our mental and physical limits, let's look at the following chart:

Chart 7

NQ (NQ Mobile Inc)
May 16 2014 01:20:56

© TC2000.com

. . . let's see how high this can go.
I'm up more than 100%.

Breakout and powerful upswing . . .

30.24

12.09

7.61

47% drop in one day

Mar   Apr   May   Jun   Jul   Aug   Sep   Oct   12/9/2013

Focus on the 47% one-day drop. That kind of price drop is not common but happens often enough that traders must always exercise strict risk management. So let's repeat: if we are going to speculate, we should do so with only a small portion of our savings.

Finally, realize that speculating is not the easier or quicker path to wealth compared to investing in an index fund or picking stocks. Trading is a different path, but we must not consider it an approach that is less serious or less demanding. I think trading well demands more patience than buying and holding for a generation or waiting years for a stock to go on sale. Why? When we trade, we constantly look at charts. The price action stimulates our brain and tempts us to trade even when not trading is the best thing to do. Every losing trade—and there will be many of them—can be a reminder of our failure that compels us to act rashly to make back the money we lost. But as with staying invested in an index fund or waiting for stock prices to come down, successful trading is also more staying still than acting. Chart patterns that launch big moves can take months or years to develop. And promising patterns often fail and reset the clock. Meanwhile, just as we must as stock pickers, we must do our homework and be ready and solvent to bet on an attractive set-up.

Chapter 11
Staying Away from Stocks

We've learned about the challenges but also the triumphant effectiveness of buying and holding an index fund. We've learned logical and safety-oriented ways to analyze stocks. And we've learned some principles of risk-limiting speculation, if we decide—after careful consideration—to trade stocks with a small portion of our savings.

Or, we could decide that getting involved in stocks—in any manner—just isn't for us.

Why would we not encourage everyone to get into stocks given the chance to multiply our savings? Why, after learning about the traps in the market and our psychology, would we even mention the option not to invest? How can we turn people away from the magic of compounding interest?

We noted in Chapter 1 how many books tout the transformative power of compound interest by saying some variation of the following:

> U.S. stocks have returned about 10% a year. If you put $100,000 in a diversified index fund when you are 35 years old, you will have more than $1.7 million 30 years later.

We, too, believe compound interest is powerful. But we also know the "details" that other books ignore. There is of course the life-long challenge of staying invested for 20 or 30 years through the market's ecstatic excesses and depressing lows. And there are other factors that affect our total return, including: the inflation rate, when an investor starts to invest, when an investor withdraws his or her money, and whether stocks will be as rewarding in the next 50 years as they have been for the past 50 years.

Then there is the following: even if stocks produce a positive return over the next 30 years, *we won't earn a positive return every year*. Stocks may go up 15% for four years straight. But they may go down double digits in back to back years and lose half or more of its value. Six years ago the market lost 56% of its value during the global financial crisis. And the market lost 90% of its value at the beginning of the Great Depression of the 1930s.

If we put $10,000 in an index fund today, we must be prepared for the possibility that we may have only $5,000 a year later. We may have 20% or 30% more, but we might also have 10%, 25%, or 50% less. Even after our money has shrunk by 50%, there is no rule that says the market must quickly recover and make us feel better. The market can continue to go down. Then it can stay down for years. And when might the market recover? Well, the market seems go up only after we can no longer take it and sell our shares to try to protect what remains. We have a remarkable ability to panic and sell at the lowest price after we boastfully buy high.

So if we are going to invest, we must *not* assume the following:

> If I put $10,000 in an index fund, then I will earn 10% every year so that I have:
>
>> $11,000 next year,
>> $12,100 in two years,
>> $13,310 in three years,
>> and so on until I have …
>> $108,000 in 25 years!

Instead, we must be ready for a jolting and sobering ride:

> If I put $10,000 in an index fund, then I must be ready to not touch this money for a long, long time. I have no idea what my investment will be worth next year. It may be

$12,000 or $8,000 or some other amount. My journey may go something like:

Year 0: $10,000
Year 1: $12,000
Year 2: $11,500
Year 3: $11,000
Year 4: $14,000
Year 5: $12,500
Year 6: $12,000
Year 7: $12,100
Year 8: $12,800
Year 9: $12,000
Year 10: $10,300
Year 11: $9,500
Year 12: $8,800
Year 13: $9,700
Year 14: $8,500
Year 15: $9,600
Year 16: $11,100
Year 17: $12,300
Year 18: $13,100
Year 19: $12,800
Year 20: $14,200
Year 21: $15,500
Year 22: $16,000
Year 23: $17,600
Year 24: $18,800
Year 25: $20,100

And if we are not open to this path as a possible, perhaps relatively fortunate, and maybe even the likely outcome, then the wise and most profitable decision is to stay out of stocks.

Put bluntly, if we do not think we can accept a 30%, 40%, or 50% or greater drop in our account at any point in our investment lifetime, then we should not be in stocks. There is no shame in admitting so and not investing. That's wisdom.

Part IV

Additional Tools

Chapter 12

Past Performance Does Not Guarantee Future Results.
Or Does it?

"This time is different"

Despite our shortcomings as investors, we tend to believe in our superior investing skill over the ancients who had to call their brokers on a landline (what's that?) to buy and sell stocks. We have the Internet, smartphones, tablet computers, and smart watches. Surely such marvels, and the even more neat things to come, justify paying expensive prices for exciting stocks. "This time is different," we proclaim, and the old rules do not apply to us because the future is brighter than ever.

Choose: Internet or flush toilet?

But let's apply our mental brakes and ask a question: if we had to choose, would we pick the Internet or the flush toilet? Of course the Inter … wait. So if we pick the Internet, does that mean we have to use an outhouse everyday? What about a choice between the Internet and indoor plumbing? Or the car? Or the light bulb? All these "old economy" inventions are more than 100 years old.

Whenever we hear that paying expensive prices for "innovative" companies is smart investing because they will change our lives, we should pause and think. Yes, life in America is more prosperous (at least materially) and healthy (at least in terms of average life expectancy) than before. But are the technologies that we hold dear in the 2010s so special? Are the gadgets that we shove into our face at the Thanksgiving gathering revolutionary in the sense that we couldn't do without them?

I don't think so. I bet more people would give up the Internet than the flush toilet, the car, or indoor plumbing. We certainly would give up our smartphone for life-saving penicillin, discovered in 1928. All this is not to bash the Internet. The Internet is amazing. Still, the point is that we are likely over-estimating—as the economist Tyler Cowen argues—the impact of the Internet and mobile technologies. This glorification is understandable. Every generation may feel they are the most enlightened. I am reminded of the saying that every generation thinks they invented sex. Well, we didn't. So let's remind ourselves of the timelessness of wisdom. Instead of dismissing safety-first rules of investing as only for our parents and grandparents, we should take them seriously.

Have we been here before?

This discussion of the Internet, the flush toilet, and the value of humility and perspective leads us to the following chart:

Chart 8

Q Ratio Since 1900

dshort.com
April 2015
Data through March

The Q Ratio is based on data from the Federal Reserve Z.1 Statistical Release, section B.102 Balance Sheet of Nonfarm Nonfinancial Corporate Business. Specifically it is the ratio of Line 39 (Corporate Equities; Liability) divided by Line 36 (Corporate Business; Net Worth). Data estimates before 1945 were provided by John Mihaljevic, Dr. Tobin's research assistant at Yale.

Source: http://www.advisorperspectives.com/dshort/updates/Q-Ratio-and-Market-Valuation.php.
Chart used with permission of Mr. Doug Short.

The Q Ratio compares the total value of the stock market versus the replacement cost of all the companies that make up the market. Replacement cost is the cost to replace an asset. For example, how much would it cost to replace Chipotle's assets if a fire destroyed them? While replacement cost is not a perfect measure, it is arguably a less fickle and more objective yardstick than the value of the stock market—which is driven by economic and company fundamentals but also by volatile swings of greed and fear.

A high Q Ratio is when the total value of the stock market is high in comparison to the cost to replace the companies that make up the market. We can think of it in the following way: when we buy stocks when the Q Ratio is at 1.08, we are paying $1.08 for every $1 of assets. We are paying 8 cents more than is necessary to replace $1 worth of assets. This "overpaying" shows the market is expensive because we are enthusiastic—likely too enthusiastic—about stocks.

In contrast, a low Q Ratio is when the stock market's value is low compared to the value of corporate assets. When we buy stocks when the Q Ratio is around 0.30, then we are in essence paying 30 cents to buy every $1 of assets—a 70% discount. Such a bargain would occur because we are pessimistic—probably excessively so—about stocks and economic prospects.

Q Ratio peaks

Over the last 100 years, the Q Ratio peaked at 1.08 in the early 1900s before a 20-year period of depressed stock prices, peaked again around 1.08 in both the late 1920s (before the Great Depression) and mid-1930s (before the Recession of 1937 to 1938), peaked at almost 1.00 in the late 1960s before the stock market started a decade-long stagnation, and peaked at 1.64 in 2000 before the crash of the dotcom bubble.

As of April 2015, the Q Ratio is at 1.11, higher than any period over the last 100 years except the years leading up to the top of the tech mania. Chart 8 shows that a Q Ratio of 1.00 or 0.90 or even 0.80 is a high level that often marked the top of the stock market before the start of a long decline.

That said, the Q Ratio is not effective as a timing tool because a high Q ratio does not predict a market decline with any precision. The Ratio can go from a high level to a higher level and continue to go up to an extremely high level as it did during the late 1990s. So while the current Q Ratio of 1.11 says the stock market is very expensive, that doesn't guarantee the market will crash next week or even next year. The market might go up for years and the Q Ratio may go higher than in 2000.

That's not to say we should go all in on stocks. Instead, we could use the Q Ratio as a big-picture indicator that tells us where the stock market stands in historical perspective. *And historical knowledge is important if only because it makes us think perhaps, just perhaps, we've been here before and nothing is new under the sun, and that we are not immune from economic cycles.*

Q Ratio has eerily bottomed at 0.30 four times

Now let's look at the low points of the Q Ratio. It bottomed at essentially 0.30 not twice, not three times, but *four times* over the last 100 years: in the early 1920s just before the stock market went on an epic run during the Roaring 20s, in the early 1930s before the stock market sharply recovered after the Depression crash, in the early 1950s as the 20-year post-World War II bull market was getting started, and in the early 1980s as the stock market was about to start the greatest stock boom in American history that lasted until 2000.

We might conclude that we should wait until the Q Ratio gets somewhere around 0.30 and then invest in stocks. But remember that the Q Ratio is not a timing tool. Just as the Q Ratio can go from expensive to more expensive (higher), it can go from inexpensive to more inexpensive (lower). That said, I would rather buy index fund shares when the Q Ratio is around 0.30 or even 0.50 than when it is 1.00 or higher.

The Q Ratio reached 0.57 in 2009: was that the generational bottom?

Notice how the Q Ratio bottomed at 0.57 in 2009 during the recent global financial crisis before recovering to the current level of 1.11.

Was it different this time and the stock market hit a long-term bottom—and set up a long-term stock boom that we are still in the middle of—at a much higher level than the previous four times? *Is there any basis to say anything was different?* Perhaps the market bottoming at 0.30 on four occasions over 100 years was coincidence and we are attributing a pattern to randomness. Even if the Q Ratio at 0.57 in 2009 was not the bottom and we are just postponing an awful crash, the Ratio can go higher for a long time. How long? Maybe until those of us sitting on the sidelines decide "we have to get into stocks."

In short, nobody knows. Yes, we can at times, such as now, say that the stock market is expensive in historical terms. But that "truth" doesn't show us a way to make money. The market does not follow a moral script. Investing based on what the market "should" or "should not" do leads to losses.

How to use the Q Ratio

So why discuss the Q ratio? For three reasons.

First, the Q Ratio gives us historical context by measuring the stock market in a rational way even if it is not a forecasting or timing tool.

Second, we need not invest at the bottom to be successful. Our investing timeline is 20 years or longer, and it is unnecessary—nor possible except by luck—to catch the bottom. Obsessing over investing at the absolute bottom means losing sight of our main and only goal: staying invested for a generation or longer.

Third, the Q Ratio is a steady reference we can check to stay grounded and sane during both market manias and depressions. It reminds us to be cautious and optimistic. Let's say we've been putting $100 a month into a low-cost index fund and then find ourselves in an euphoric stock boom that has elevated stock prices to historically high levels as measured by the Q Ratio. Investment gurus and friends urge us to buy that latest hot stock and go all in on the market to make easy money. Tempting, but we apply our mental brakes. We look at the Q Ratio to get a sense of where the market stands against history. Let's say that the ratio is at 1.11, where it was as of April 2015. That's expensive. We know it is the second highest level in over 100 years. So we politely decline the advice of our well-meaning friends. We continue to buy index fund shares every month but we don't chase stocks that are selling at expensive levels despite middling prospects and shaky balance sheets. We stay above the market frenzy by setting our investment program on cruise control and ignoring the day-to-day and even the year-to-year fluctuations.

And should the market crash and the Q Ratio again decline steeply, perhaps to 0.30 again, and none of our friends want anything to do with stocks, then we might remember the resilience of Americans and the U.S. economy and continue, and perhaps even increase, our regular investment.

Just one thing—staying the course—will mean we'll likely compile a record that will be the envy of everyone. Adding one more act of gumption—buying more index fund shares during the darkest moments when others are panicking—will make us anonymous great investors.

Chapter 13
We Must Always Ask This Question

Let's say we are considering buying the neighborhood ice cream store. We consider its customer base, competition, and prospects. And of course we want to know how much money it makes in a year. We consider these factors against the selling price and decide whether it makes sense to buy this store. These considerations also apply when we are thinking about buying shares in a multi-billion dollar company like Chipotle. We consider Chipotle's customer reviews, competition, brand story, and financials.

Yet we tend to ditch all rational business inquiries when investing in the stock market. For some reason we think basic financial considerations don't apply when investing in a big company. And one of the most important questions that we ignore—or that we are not even aware of—is: *how much should we pay for every $1 profit made by Chipotle?* After all, we would not pay more than a certain amount to buy the ice cream store no matter how charming and profitable it may be. Why wouldn't the same business sense apply to a stock investment?

Let's start with the ice cream store to illustrate this concept.

How much might we pay for an ice cream store making $100,000 a year?

Say the ice cream shop makes $100,000 a year after taxes and all expenses. What's this store worth? Assuming a good location with a stable earnings history and good prospects for continued profitability, let's say we would pay $400,000.

Another way of looking at it is by asking how much we would pay for every $1 profit that the ice cream store makes. By valuing the store at $400,000, we are willing to pay $4 for every $1 of income. In the language of the stock market, we are giving the store a price-to-earnings (or "P/E") ratio of 4 and we are valuing the store at four times its earnings (called the earnings multiple). We divided $400,000 (the "P" or Price) by $100,000 (the "E" or Earnings) to get 4. The higher the P/E ratio, the more we are paying for every dollar of a store or company's annual income.

We can and must apply this concept to any investment. Let's apply it to Chipotle.

How much does a person buying a share of Chipotle today pay for every $1 that Chipotle earned last year?

Chipotle made $445 million in the most recent 12-month period as of April 2015 and the company is valued at about $21 billion. We divide $21 billion (the "P" or the Price) by $445 million (the "E" or Earnings) and get approximately 47. If we wish to invest in Chipotle, we have to pay $47 for every $1 that Chipotle earned. Investors are giving Chipotle a P/E ratio of 47 and valuing the company at 47 times its earnings.

Why is the ice cream shop valued at only four times its earnings while Chipotle is valued—at least currently—47 times its income? One reason is that small businesses are generally valued at a lower earnings multiple than large public companies like Chipotle. Small businesses make less money and are not as stable as multi-billion dollar global corporations (although big businesses face intense competition and their survival is never guaranteed). Another reason is that publicly-traded companies like Chipotle can be subject to public adoration that pushes up the stock price and P/E ratio to a much higher level. We'll discuss this possibility in a bit. But regardless of the difference in the scale of profits and sales, all businesses can be analyzed using the P/E ratio.

Say the average multiple paid for a small business is around 3 to 5 (P/E ratio of 3 to 5). This range is a useful reference against which we can evaluate the attractiveness of buying a business. If a sandwich shop in a charming shopping area making a profit of $100,000 a year is selling at $200,000 (P/E ratio of 2, or twice its earnings), then we may conclude that this store—if it meets other requirements such as a stable earnings history and good prospects—may be an attractive investment.

The same analysis applies to a large public company like Chipotle. Over the long run, the average P/E ratio of the overall stock market has been around 15. That is, on average over the last 100 years, investors paid about $15 for every $1 of income earned by companies in the stock market. Now we have some point of reference by which to judge the expensiveness—and thus risk—of a stock such as Chipotle. Where does Chipotle stand with its growing business and low debt but a high P/E ratio of 47 and a stock price more than 10 times its book value?

Would we pay $4.7 million for an ice cream store making $100,000 a year?

Graham recommended that we consider investing in a stock whose P/E ratio is no more than 15 times the average earnings of the past three years (in addition to other requirements such a strong balance sheet and good prospects). Why the average of three years? Because a company can have one unusually good year and thus increase its "E" and shrink its P/E ratio and give the appearance that it is a bargain investment. Many companies can pull off a good year or a couple of good years, especially in a booming economy. Fewer companies can grow or maintain its earnings for five or more years. In fact, Graham urges us to consider the average earnings of the past 10 years to get a sense of a company's true profitability. Looking back a decade we get a sense of how a company performs during tough economic times and not just boom times.

Chipotle's P/E ratio of 47 is much too high compared to Graham's general cutoff at 15. If we pay $47 for $1 of Chipotle's income, we are essentially saying we hope Chipotle will grow faster and earn more than the already-high forecasts. In other words, an idealized future must come true and there is no margin of error, and thus no margin of safety.

I come to this conclusion as a fan. Chipotle is my first choice for a fast-food meal. Sure, Chipotle may pull it off. But it may not. Failing to grow as rapidly as today's investors hope does not mean Chipotle will fail as a business. Graham is not saying that a company whose stock has a high P/E ratio is a bad company. In fact, it is probably a good and growing company. That's why people are excited about the stock and have bid it up to an expensive price. But good companies are often bad investments because we must pay such a high price that there is no margin of safety. Chipotle may be the best-run chain restaurant in the world today. ***But the sober business question remains***: would the intelligent investor pay so much over book value and over $47 for $1 of earnings to own a slice of Chipotle? Reasonable minds can differ, but my answer—and probably Graham's response—is no.

Let's revisit a quote from *The Intelligent Investor* that we discussed in Chapter 9:

> A stock investment made not too far above a company's book value "may with logic be regarded as related to the company's balance sheet and as having support independent of fluctuating market prices." An investor who makes such an investment "can take a much more independent and detached view of stock-market fluctuations than those who have paid high multiples of both earnings and book value."

If we buy Chipotle shares with a P/E ratio of 47 and at 10 times book value, could we stick with our "investment" through price declines of 30%, 40%, or 50% and more? The price of Chipotle shares declined by almost 50% in 2012. Sure, the stock has since gone up more than 250%. But would we have held through the 2012 crash? And would we hold through a similar or deeper decline knowing that much of Chipotle's formerly high stock price consisted of the weak commitment of other shareholders (many of whom chased the stock) and hopes of almost-perfect business execution?

Waiting for Chipotle to go on sale

But if we wait and have the chance to invest in Chipotle when its stock has a P/E ratio of, say, 13 and is selling not so far above its book value, and we also have the courage (and savings) to act after careful analysis (does Chipotle have a strong balance sheet? does it still have good prospects? is it making money in tough times?), then we have a much better chance to stay invested through the unavoidable volatility.

Consider the following hypothetical companies:

- Company A is a well-managed company in a somewhat boring industry (chemicals) with a stable history of solid earnings (it has not lost money in the past 10 years), a strong balance sheet, and good prospects with a P/E ratio of 12. Its share price is 160% of book value.

- Company B is in a flashier industry (mobile communications). It has increased its earnings in each of the past five years and is growing rapidly. It captures much media attention and is a popular growth stock. Its P/E ratio is 40 and stock price is 1200% of book value.

I would invest in Company A over Company B every time. But there's a problem. Opportunities like Company A do not come up often, while "opportunities" like Company B are more common. Thus, we must have discipline and patience. Just because our checklist disqualifies most stocks from investment does not mean our approach is wrong. It means we choose to emphasize safety over potential, facts over hype, and a tough business mindset over a hunch.

Bring a business mindset—not emotion and hype—to the stock market

Let's return to our ice cream shop. We might pay $300,000 or so to buy it. Paying about 3 times earnings seems reasonable and fair for a small business with steady earnings and good prospects in a nice neighborhood. But we wouldn't pay 20 times ($2 million) or 15 times ($1.5 million) or even 10 times ($1 million) earnings. If we pay $1 million, we would have to make $100,000 a year for 10 years just to break even. Meanwhile, too many things can happen. Tastes change. The neighborhood can change and customers disappear. Or a larger competitor with lower prices can steal business.

If we wouldn't buy the ice cream shop at 10 or even five times its earnings, then we shouldn't be so eager to buy shares of a company—no matter how well managed and how much potential it has and even taking into account the higher valuation of public companies—at close to 50 times its earnings. Yet people who would never buy the ice cream shop at five or even four times earnings would do just that.

Is it fair or meaningful to compare an ice cream store with Chipotle? Yes. As we noted, the scale may be different, but the principle is the same. No rational person would pay any amount for a business. *There is a point at which the price paid becomes too expensive and too risky. Reasonable minds may disagree as to where that line is drawn, but it is better to err on the side of safety*—and Graham's approach shows us how. Why did Graham emphasize safety and caution so much? Temperament and personal style are likely factors. Personal experience was also a factor as Graham lost almost everything during the Great Depression. Afterwards he said:

> Some hard experience taught [me] it was better to be safe
> and careful rather than try to make all the money in the
> world.

Anything can happen. Competition. Mismanagement. Changing customer tastes. Higher prices for ingredients. A recession. A depression. As investors we have no control over these things. But we have control over how much we pay for a stock.

An understandable complaint is that after more than six years of rising stock prices as of May 2015, there doesn't seem to be any stocks that pass Graham's strict tests. If there are attractive investment opportunities, perhaps it takes extraordinary judgment to sniff them out: the kind of stock-picking skill possessed by only a few. Then it may be that we are left with investing in and holding low-cost index funds (for the long run, of course) or simply staying out.

Remember, we do not have to be in stocks just because we know more about the market than most people. That's one of the paradoxes of investing. The more we know, the more we realize nothing is simple in the stock market. Also remember that we *are* applying our knowledge by deciding not to invest. Graham's methods and even the principles of responsible speculation are most valuable as tools of caution and risk management that *eliminate* stocks from investment or trade consideration. That often means doing nothing, just like a buy-and-hold-forever index-fund investor.

Doing nothing is hard work

And that's the challenge: we are impatient and doing nothing is hard work. If quick profits are the goal, then we will fail as index fund investors, stock pickers, and traders. To succeed, we need more patience, self-awareness, and perspective than we have now. And so, ironically, the non-financial rewards of adopting timeless virtues is perhaps one reason why we might enter the worldly arena of stocks. We have to be in it for more than money.

Part V

Final Thoughts

Chapter 14
First We Must Do This

No gain is so certain as that which
proceeds from the economical use of
what you already have.

Latin proverb

This chapter is the shortest and the most fundamental.

We must live within our means and become savers before we become index fund investors, stock pickers, or equity traders. While investing is one way we can use our savings, investing—let alone stock picking or speculating—is not our fundamental aim. The goal is maturity, discipline, patience, and self-reliance. That these qualities will help us become better investors is just a secondary benefit of the unshakable power and dignity of financial responsibility. And it is never too late to start saving.

I sometimes hear from people who are eager to buy stocks that stocks are the best way to increase our savings. I disagree. If we have $5000 in savings and our goal is to have $7,500 in savings by the end of the year, then let's consider some ways we can increase our savings by $2,500 or 50%, an admirable accomplishment. We can put our entire savings in the stock market and hope that stocks go up 50% in a year. This "strategy" is at best risky and unrealistic.

Instead, saving is the surer way we can increase our savings by 50% in a year. The difficulty of saving $2,500 on, say, a $40,000 income will depend on, for example, whether we have a family and whether emergency expenses come up. Whatever our circumstances, living within our means will give us the best chance to reach our savings goal.

We do not have to be in stocks to live an abundant, independent, and full life. We must never forget that living within our means is the always available way to secure our financial future.

Chapter 15
Conclusion

If we are successful as investors, our market wealth will be earned over the long run. The irony is that perhaps the best way to invest in an index fund—which is the main way we should approach stocks—is to invest and forget: to be too busy living life, spending time with family and friends, and building things to care about the market.

Our journey through the stock market has stressed restraint, self-awareness, and perspective over excitement, hype, and pursuit. We learned about the traps and frustrations of the market that others don't discuss. And we learned the paramount importance of patience. Whether buying-and-holding an index fund for decades without meddling, eliminating expensive stocks from investment consideration and waiting until attractive prices are available, or speculating only when the charts show a set-up worth betting on, sitting still is often key.

We should participate in the stock market only after careful study and self-examination. Humility, detachment, and independence are vital whether we become an indexer, stock picker, trader, some combination thereof, or none of the above. If we decide to participate in the market, we will find that the non-financial requirements and rewards of intelligent investing and trading are most meaningful and valuable.

About the Author

Brian is an investor, market analyst, teacher, academic consultant, writer, and classical chartist. He has written about equity returns and corporate governance for publications such as the *Harvard Journal on Legislation* and has been interviewed by the financial site MainStreet.com. Brian is also the author of *Trading Stocks Using Classical Chart Patterns: A Complete Tactical and Psychological Guide for Beginners and Experienced Traders.*

You can follow Brian at classicalchartist.blogspot.com for frequent chart analyses and on Twitter @BrianKimmer.

Brian studied at the University of California at Berkeley and at Harvard Law School and was a Harvard Law School Post-Graduate Research Fellow. Brian welcomes readers to get in touch at brian.b.kim@gmail.com.

Disclaimer

Everything in this book is for educational purposes only and is not to be considered professional advice of any kind. All statements and opinions in this book are not meant to be a solicitation or recommendation to buy, sell, or hold securities. Investing and trading involve risk of loss.

www.ingramcontent.com/pod-product-compliance
Lightning Source LLC
Chambersburg PA
CBHW060630210326
41520CB00010B/1550